An Address, Delivered Before The
Association Of Teachers, And Friends Of
Popular Education: By S. H. Blake

S. H. Blake

In the interest of creating a more extensive selection of rare historical book reprints, we have chosen to reproduce this title even though it may possibly have occasional imperfections such as missing and blurred pages, missing text, poor pictures, markings, dark backgrounds and other reproduction issues beyond our control. Because this work is culturally important, we have made it available as a part of our commitment to protecting, preserving and promoting the world's literature. Thank you for your understanding.

AN

ADDRESS,

DELIVERED BEFORE THE

ASSOCIATION OF TEACHERS,

AND

FRIENDS OF POPULAR EDUCATION,

AT EXETER, DEC. 28, 1836.

BY S. H. BLAKE.

BANGOR:
PUBLISHED BY THE ASSOCIATION.
S. S. SMITH, PRINTER.
1837.

ADDRESS.

Different ages have been characterised by different features. At one time, literature and science have flourished—commerce has been extended—and the arts of civilized life have been cultivated. At another, the love of military acievements has held the public mind captive—the desire of conquest and of empire has had the ascendency—and the arts of husbandry and peace have been neglected and forgotten. At one time, the path of the orator and poet has been strewn with flowers by an admiring populace—at another the return of the warrior from conquered provinces has been honored with triumphal arches.

At one time, too, a long night of darkness set in upon the world, and the light of learning and science glimmered only in the convent and the cloister—then, long after the power of Roman arms had ceased, Roman literature again revived. Her collected learning that had been scattered, at the time of her subjugation, through the north of Europe, and nearly extinguished, was now again rekindled and spread like wild-fire throughout the continent. Ignorance was dispelled—science threw off its shackles;—and more—the stone was rolled back from the tomb of christianity, and she arose in the might and divinity of her nature—and the *Reformation burst* upon the world. The night of darkness was gone, and a day of light succeeded.

Now, whether the tone and character of an age are given it by its own master spirits, or whether its leading features are produced by political revolutions, is a matter of most interesting examination, but which we have not time here to discuss; still, certain it is, that every age has its strong points, that stand out in bold relief, prominent as the mountain upon the landscape.

That feature in our own times is the *spirit of reform*. Old opinions are questioned and given up, and new ones adopted, in their stead—old habits of life are lain aside, like a worn out garment. Men feel restrained by the usages of their fathers and discard them as idle and useless—and invent new projects of business and of pleasure;—and principles however long and well settled, are examined anew. A spirit of *enquiry* has gone out into the world penetrating the depths and recesses of society and ascending its highest places. And the *question* is, now, every day presented to our consideration, whether this or that principle is expedient or well founded—whether this or that institution cannot be given up and a better one substituted in its place.

England has felt its influence. Her Court of Chancery has been renovated. Catholic emancipation has been yielded. The rotten Borough system has, to a degree, been given up. And the *Reform* of Parliament is the watchword of party. Free principles are insinuating themselves into her institutions, and she is every day giving way, more and more to the spirit of the age. The other governments of Europe are introducing the improvements of the day and avail themselves of every discovery in the arts and sciences, as a means of ameliorating the condition of their poor, or of promoting the common weal. In our own country as well as elsewhere, more of science than heretofore is applied to every thing, and every thing is, therefore, undergoing a change. The nature of soils and products and the effect of climate upon both, have been investigated and the agricultural interests of the country are, therefore, improving. Science has been applied to machinery, and improvements, therefore, made, that save an immense amount of manual labor, thus, leaving the operative, time to cultivate his mind or to aid in developing further, the resources of the land. Men are examining every thing, changing every thing, and we hope, improving every thing.

This spirit of reform, too, is pushed by an energy—the energy of public opinion, that it is idle to resist, if you would. You might as well stop the swell of the ocean. It is nerved by a power that no human arm can stay. It has already reached the *State* and the *Church*. It has extended its hand upon the country and upon the city—everywhere. Institutions, however hallowed by time, or however sacred from the ceremonies thrown around them have not been exempted from its touch.

But whether this spirit of the age will eventuate in good or evil, is left to the future to disclose. I apprehend, however, no danger from it. For, though, it may disturb many of our earliest and most cherished recollections—though it may sweep away many idle usages around which, nevertheless, cling many of our most interesting associations, it will yet leave room for more useful principles in their stead. It may be like a great river, in its onward and onward current, sweeping away every obstacle that opposes its course, yet safely floating upon its bosom the treasures of the world—or washing away the beautiful shrubbery, from its banks, to open a vein of gold.

I have made these remarks, to illustrate the leading feature of the times in which we live and to show the position we occupy—to show, also, that however permanent we may imagine our institutions to be, yet that a change may come over them—and that, therefore, it is our duty to place around them all the safeguards we can—to show, further, that, though we live in the full enjoyment of civil and religious liberty, yet that the sun of freedom and christianity, that now sheds its clear and strong light upon us, may by and by go down in the west. And that, therefore, the spirit of the age, and the institutions under which we live, alike impose responsibilities upon us, little less, than were assumed by our fathers, in their struggle to gain that independence, which it is our duty to preserve. And how can we discharge these high responsibilities—how can we perform our duty, as citizens, our duty, as men, our duty as legatees of a rich inheritance from our fathers, half so well as in spreading far and wide that " popular education," it is the object of this association to disseminate—and how can we diffuse this " popular education" half so well as by encouraging our " common schools?"

Our common schools are republican in their origin and in their tendency. They are in accordance with the genius of our government and with the utilitarian spirit of the day. Their great object is the diffusion of useful knowledge in the mass of society. And if they are not adequate to give the scholar, a complete education—they are sufficient to enable him to attain all that knowledge, that, ordinarily comes into use in the common business of life. And their advantages extend alike to all—so, that, every child in a neighborhood, or a town, may avail itself of the privilege of attending them, without charge, and thus, receive an education at the public expense. There is no aristocracy, no monopoly about them—but every one—the mass of society, may be educated in them. This is their object,— the education not of the *few*, not of the *rich*, not of the *poor*,—but of all—an object, upon the success of which I humbly apprehend, depends the prosperity of our free institutions and of the blessings we enjoy under them.

And it is in this point of view, the importance of our common schools is more clearly seen—if they are the medium, through which is diffused into the mass of society that general knowledge, which is necessary to the preservation of our free institutions, then they surely, are of vital consequence, and should occupy a prominent place in the patronage and legislation of government.

And this is the idea I wish to illustrate, that the education of the mass of community, for which common schools are so well adapted, is the very point upon which the perpetuity of our Republic depends. For if our government is the best practicable one that can be adopted, and every citizen is sufficiently enlightened to realize its advantages, he will use his exertions to preserve and continue it,—but however perfect it may be, if its citizens are, through ignorance, blind to its benefits, they may pull it down though it bury them in its ruins.

But this view of the *conservative* power of a general diffusion of knowledge, I fear is not duly appreciated, yet to an American citizen it is its most important view. The *common* advantages of education—its effect upon individual character or upon society at large, are too obvious for illustration and would derive no force from repetition. The divinity of our nature, that it discloses and the destination of the soul, that, aided by revelation, it points out, are momentous truths, but yet conceded. Education is, too, to the moral what the sun is to the natural world, throwing its genial rays upon the whole face of society—yet its sunny influence is seen and felt and acknowledged by all. But the bearing of this popular education upon our political institutions and the effect of our free schools upon our republican form of government, are matters, the importance of which few realize and to which in my humble estimation, our public men have not attached their due importance. For, if our free common schools are the result of the same principles, operating upon the same character, that led to the revolution and the establishment of a free government—yet they exert back upon these principles an influence, without the aid of which, the principles themselves would soon lose their force and their virtue. And these same principles that originated, are now necessary to preserve, our republican institutions. Our free schools are in this respect like the beacon lights upon our coast—themselves, the result of commerce, yet, now, the very means of preserving that commerce. The ship, laden with its treasures, as it nears our rugged shores, might be lost in their dangerous navigation, were it not for the light ahead—to guide it safely to the haven of its destination. So, too, with the ship of State, as she careers her way proudly onward, laden with the last and best hopes of freedom,—she may, still, be enveloped in darkness and be wrecked, if the clear noon-day light of popular education, thrown all around by our free schools, is withdrawn.

I have said that the diffusion of general knowledge in the mass of society is necessary to the maintenance of our liberties,—and the history of other republics more than justifies the remark.

The French republic, in our own day, though, with the American model before it, was a miserable failure. There was enough of the spirit of liberty, for it had been caught from across the Atlantic—there was enough of chivalry, for the flower of France had been educated to arms, but the nation was not prepared for the change—the public mind was not sufficiently enlightened—nor had it received the necessary moral culture.

The governments of South America, too, have alternately been free and despotic, vacillating between republics and monarchies, as the light of learning, or the darkness of ignorance alternately struggled into the ascendency. And notwithstanding their proximity to our North American confederacy and their interchange of trade and letters with us, I fear it is reserved for another day than our own, to welcome them to a participation in the great blessings of liberty that we enjoy. They have not been educated for freedom. Their priesthood may be learned, or a fortunate few enlightened—but the common mind is yet enveloped in darkness and superstition. The many have not had their eyes opened to the bright vision of liberty. And until society, there, shall have undergone a thorough reformation—until a flood of moral and mental light shall have been let in upon it—we can have little reason to expect that a popular government will be established, that shall continue any considerable length of time,—as heretofore, they may play up upon the political horison but it will be like the northern lights, when the sun of liberty is not in the heavens, and attracting the curiosity of the world, rather than justifying any well founded hope of their permanency.

The republics of classic antiquity owe their downfal to much the same causes. It is true the theory of a free government was not then well defined—the science of politics had not made much progress—the principles of civil liberty were not rightly understood. The admirable idea of dividing the legislative department into two chambers, does not seem to have been known in Greece,—and the system of the check and balance of powers, as essential to a government, as to a complicated machine, was either not known in Greece or Rome, or badly applied. But it was not political science alone, that was wanting—the theory of the government was better than the foundation upon which it rested. The foundation was unstable, for it was not based deep enough in the moral and mental improvement of the common mind.

Indeed the annals of every republic in the world, give full and conclusive evidence of the truth of the position I am attempting to illustrate.—They prove more, for while they establish this position—they also prove, that society with the degree of intelligence of which I am speaking, will always claim its rights of government and have its part in the administration of it. The spirit of liberty in however enlightened a community, may, to be sure, be overawed by military force—or it may, naturally enough, be checked in its career by the fondness, with which a people, always cling to the institutions under which they were born, but, sooner or later, in every country where the public mind is so far advanced, as to appreciate the advantages of civil and religious liberty, a government of the people will be established, and its duration will depend upon the continuance of the causes that gave it birth.

If such are the consequences of "popular education"—if such is its creative power in building up a free government and if such is its conservative influence in protecting it, I need not appeal to you as members of this association in behalf of the great object we have in view, but I should rather call upon you as citizens of the republic under which we live, to perform your duty, merely, in keeping good the inheritance, that has been left us.

Again, This view of the influence of popular education upon our Institutions, derives much force from the importance, that has ever been attached to it by our fathers. The encouragement of learning was with them, always, a prominent object. Their attention was early directed to it, and in all their struggles for independence, they never lost sight of it—almost every Constitution in the Union, bears upon its face the declaration, that "the diffusion of knowledge and learning throughout a community is essential to the preservation of the rights and liberties of a people."—And the legislation under this declaration has generally been worthy of free and sovereign States. But we may in New England go further back than to our State Constitutions, further back, even than to the Revolution, to find the interests of science and literature recognized and cherished. The Puritan Pilgrims had hardly landed upon the rock-bound coast of the wilderness of Plymouth, when their attention was directed to the education of their children. Indeed, this was a leading inducement to their emigration to this country. They had already become exiles from their native land for conscience sake and had settled at Leyden in Holland—where they could worship God in their own way. But they found, to use their own language "that the place being of great " licentiousness and liberty to children, *they could* " *not educate them*, nor could they give them due " correction, without reproof or reproach from their neighbors." They wished therefore to settle in another Land, where the prospects of their posterity might be more encouraging. But they sought, in the beautiful phrase of another, not merely a " faith's pure shrine" but liberty to educate their children, as they pleased, without reproach or restraint.

The Pilgrims landed in the *May Flower*, in the fall of 1620—forty four of their number, which was one hundred and one, died before the end of the March following. This melancholy event, and then, the cheerless prospect ahead, would have disheartened any men under heaven, other than the

simple, yet stern Puritans of that day. But they on the contrary, persevered with a rigor and an energy, that has ever since given a tone to New-England character. Hence we find them, with a singleness of purpose that at this distance of time, appears more like fiction than reality, making early provision for the promotion of religion and learning. By an early ordinance of the general court of Plymouth, it was provided "that the prof-
"its arising to the Colony by the above said fishing
"at the Cape (referring to Cape Cod) shall be em-
"ployed and improved for the erecting and main-
"taining of a free school in this government." This was the germ of our New England system of free schools.—The Colony of Massachusetts Bay, too, in 1635 only five years after any considerable settlement there, had a free school in Boston—and in 1644 one town resolved to devote a portion of its Lands to the support of schools—a good evidence of the general interest in the matter,—and in 1647 a general provision was made by the Colony for a free school in every town "after that the Lord in-
"creased them to fifty house holders" and for the setting up of a "grammar school" "when any town
"shall increase to the number of one hundred
"house holders or families." From these provisions of the colonies of Plymouth and Massachusetts was evolved and established this great element of modern society, our free schools.—A school, supported at the expence of government—free to all the children of the community—in other words the proposition, that it is the duty of the *State to educate its own children*, was a simple idea. But it was here for the first time conceived. It originated in the

peculiar character and polity of the colonies. And however simple it may now seem, it is a conception, that, in its future progress and developement, is calculated to have more influence upon the destiny of the world, than any other principle or institution, save only that of christianity itself. It was indeed a discovery—and if the announcement of a new world by Columbus was more startling to the ear, it was hardly destined to be more important in its consequences. In coming times it will be looked upon, as marking the era—and the age.—And this, gentlemen, is the Institution, thus originated and thus founded that it is the object of this Association to encourage,—to improve—and to protect.

I have given my remarks so far, more of a political cast, and it may be a wider range than the occasion at first blush might seem to justify. I have not, however, I believe, given to " popular education" any thing more than its legitimate influence. And if not, the enquiry, paramount to all others, is, how we can best promote it—and if by our common schools, whether they can be improved and whether they have kept pace with the advance of the day.

Our schools may, perhaps, be improved by elevating the character of the master—by a more judicious selection of agents and school committees—by a greater regard in the construction of school rooms to the convenience and health of the student—by introducing better and more apparatus for the illustration of principles—by introducing other and better books—by holding out to the scholar higher and more encouraging motives to study. The mind may perhaps, be more cheered in its progress, more encouraged in its attainments, and more applauded in its success. Meetings of the scholars for public reading, at which parents should attend, and then, the bestowal of some mark of approbation upon the best readers, might conduce to improvement in this important branch. Public discussion every week, in which the more advanced of the scholars, the master, and parents, might all take a part—might inspire confidence—give a command of language,—and elicit talent that would otherwise have lain dormant. But upon the particular management of schools and the mode of instruction, I yield with deference to those, who have had these matters under their more immediate charge.

A remark, however, may be here made of much consequence, and it is this, that the benefit of a school to the scholars very much depends upon the estimation in which it is held by the parents. If the parent encourage the child—if he aid and assist the master—if he feel the importance of having the twig bent in the right direction—if he realizes, that the future usefulness, and even success in life—and more, the very character of the child, may depend upon its earliest impressions at school. If, in fine, he look upon the school, as the place where his sons may lay the foundation of that knowledge and after greatness, that shall fit them for the highest places of honor and trust—and where his daughters may receive that education, that shall adorn and please—and where they shall have induced upon their minds that love of virtue and that consciousness of the dignity of their sex, that shall fit them so to bring up their own children that like the mother of the Grachii, they may proudly point to them, as their jewels—if, I say, parents will thus regard our schools—their benefits will be greatly enhanced—the progress of the scholar advanced—and the task of the master alleviated.

Another suggestion, quite as important to my own mind is, whether, the writings of American authors may not with eminent propriety be more read and studied in our schools than they are. Our literature needs the pecuniary aid and encouragement it would thus receive and its merits entitle it to this favourable countenance. It is already rich in its language, its sentiment and its matter, and is assuming a high character,—it is, to be sure, new, but then it breathes the free and vigorous spirit of our institutions. And our whole country and our whole history too, are full of precisely those materials—of wild and beautiful scenery—of anecdote and story and thrilling event, that are fitted to charm the youthful imagination and to impart interest and profit to the maturer judgment. Our early colonial settlement—our Indian wars—our disasters and successes—our struggle for independence against fearful odds—the story of the revolution, the battles, that did honor to American chivalry and that have so often been fought over again in the chimney corner—are all full of stirring incident—and well calculated to arrest and fix the attention of the youthful reader, and far more so, than the chapter of kings or the overthrow of petty dynasties. And the study of our own history would have this advantage, that it would inspire a love of country, and give an American tone to the feelings.—Further, it would do more—as the youth should carry his imagination back to the struggle of our fathers and identify himself with the scenes, that were then acting, he would see the first blood that was shed in the war of the revolution, poured out upon the fields of Lexington—he would see a brave band upon the heights of Bunker Hill, and would there mourn the untimely death of the gallant Warren—he would see the long and unequal and doubtful struggle for freedom—and his heart would beat quicker with the aspirations of liberty, and he would better know how to value the inheritance of his fathers.—It is, again, to be considered that our common schools afford to very many, their only means of acquiring a knowledge of the principles of our government and of the structure of our society before going out into the world, to assume the responsibilities and to discharge the duties, of citizens and voters—and, that, if their education in this respect is then neglected they may either imbibe foreign notions hostile to liberty—or, be placed in situations where through ignorance they may jeopard their dearest rights. May it not, then, be well, to guard against the one by inspiring an early attachment to our own institutions, and to avoid the other by inculcating an early knowledge of their principles? If the history of the old world, with its shipwrecked republics strewn all along upon its shores, be instructive to the politician—if its literature, graced by an Augustan or a Elizabethan age, be stored with intellectual wealth for the scholar—if its castles and strong holds, tumbled into ruins, and grown over with ivy, have charms for the antiquary—may not their study, however interesting, be well postponed, till the chart of our own shores shall have been examined, to ascertain its rocks and quicksands—till one draught, at least, of the fresh and bracing spirit of our own letters shall have been inhaled—till something shall have been learned of the when and where and how our own republic came into being?—It appears to me, that the American youth, while learning to read, even, should also be learning the history of his country, his government and his fathers—that he should be learning something of the causes that led to the throwing off our colonial subjugation, and to the establishment of our liberties—something of the difficulties under which the confederation laboured, and the consequent necessity, and yet the embarrassment that attended the formation, of a new constitution, and then its operation—that, he might thereby get an insight into the theory of our government and its practical effects, and thus be better able duly to appreciate the blessings he enjoyed under it, or better fitted to take a part in its administration, if the interests of his country should require.—If it should be said that we have no work of merit, suited to our common schools, that would answer these purposes, I can only reply that it is then time we had, for it could not be otherwise than salutary in the interest it would excite in the reading, and in the impression it would leave upon the mind.

But while we would improve the intellectual, we must not forget the moral faculties. The capacities of the mind all require to be cultivated, in order that it may unfold itself in its full beauty and power. The mind is here, wrapped in its human covering, in its chrysalis state, having within itself the germs of all its after hopes and aspirations—but its every capacity must be aided, if when it throws off this covering, you would have it have strength of wing enough to soar to the place of its high destination. Its every power must be developed to give it perfection.—It is true, the distinction between the moral and intellectual faculties cannot be well defined—for they blend together like light and shade—and act upon each other with a mysterious sympathy. They have however, the character of checks upon each other—and it must have attracted the observation of every one, that the cultivating the one class of faculties, to the entire neglect of the other, has always thrown the mind from its balance and been prejudicial in its consequences. But when a due regard has been had to a proper culture of both classes of faculties—the effect has, ever, been happy and salutary. Society bears proof of this all around us—upon its very face and in its very condition and character. But an illustration, more striking from its contrast may be found in a higher sphere—in the life of him, whose ashes are entombed upon the banks of the Potomac, and whose memory is the common property of freemen, the world over.

The mind of Washington was of an high order and the best evidence of it is, that he was not above the common details and business of life. He lived with men, as men, and availed himself of all their aid to effect, what seemed to be the great object of his life, the promotion of the greatest public good. In the camp, he consulted with his companions in arms and maturely weighed their suggestions before forming or acting upon his own opinion—in the councils of State, he advised with men best acquainted with the subject under consideration and cheerfully availed himself of all the knowledge they possessed, to aid him in his deliberations,—in the camp and in the cabinet, he was therefore wise and successful.—And the secret of his greatness and his usefulness was in the due balance of his moral and intellectual faculties. They were cherished together, acquired strength together, and together lent their aid in giving vigor and maturity to his mind. Like mechanical powers they united to give his mind additional impetus—propelling it ahead and yet not thereby endangering its safety—for neither had strength enough to push it off in a tangent, but acting together, they kept it balanced and in its place.— And hence, receiving at the hands of nature a commanding mind, he became a great man—inducing upon that mind, proper moral culture, he became a good man—and his whole life was but an illustration of this character. Long since his spirit took wing for heaven, but his memory is yet fresh in the hearts of a greatful people and when if ever, we may be called upon, to mourn the downfal of our republic—then, and not till then, may his memory be forgotten.

Upon the other hand, to show the effect of intellectual culture upon character without due moral improvement, observe if you will the career of another like master spirit—I refer to him, whose bones now lie mouldering in the Island of St. Helena.——To be sure the qualities of mind, that enabled Napoleon to dazzle the world with the splendor of his military achievements, were not strictly intellectual, yet they presupposed a high state of mental improvement. His taste for the fine arts, even, shew itself in his first campaign in Italy, for by his direction, a victorious army returned laden with the finest specimens of Italian sculpture and painting. And in Egypt, he gave evidence of the same inclination of mind, for he caused drawings and plans to be made of whatever he found remarkable in their public works or curious in their hyerogliphical inscriptions—of their mounds and monuments—of their temples and their gods,—indeed, of every thing, that threw light upon the antiquities of that ancient people or tended to illustrate the then and past state of the arts and sciences in that interesting country.— It is a rare work, and I am not aware that there is more than one copy in this county. But it is a monument, showing the intellectual bias of his mind, that will be preserved in the archives of science, as long as his unprovoked attack upon that country will be reprobated and regretted by the world. But his splendid works of internal improvement and among others the road over the Simplon, his collecting together at Paris every thing beautiful in the arts and sciences that the world afforded, his reducing the administration of justice in the different provinces to a uniform system—and lastly the code of laws that bears his name, and that will cause it to live, too, in the memory of the great and wise, long after the story of Waterloo and Moscow shall be forgotten—a code of laws, singular as it may seem, that with a few modifications has been adopted by one of the States of our own Union— all these, are proud evidences of his intellectual greatness, and if dimmed at all by the glare of his military career, they only show the more the mighty compass of his mind. And yet it had been better for the world, that Napoleon had never been born.

For his career was a career of usurpation and bloodshed. His victories were a succession of unwarranted attacks upon nations with which France was at peace. He trampled, with impunity, upon the rights of man, and the usages of society—at one time contemning whatever was virtuous and pious, and at another, setting up a mockery of religion, for State purposes. He knocked together the thrones of Europe and tumbled them into the dust, not that the people might be happier, or society improved and ameliorated in its condition, but that his own personal aggrandizement might thereby be promoted.—Now, had the mind of Napoleon from infancy up been under the moral restraint, that checked the aspiring powers of Washington—had an early love of virtue been instilled into his mind, a regard for truth and duty and religion been inculcated—in fine had his mental and moral faculties gone hand in hand in their progress, he might have been, and from his peculiar position, probably, would have been a great, acknowledged benefactor of human society, and the world would have owed him a debt of gratitude—and more, his own idolized France might at this day have been free and republican, and have revered his memory as the Father of his country. But I need not, as I said before, have gone out of the sphere of your own immediate observation, to have illustrated the influence of moral education upon individual character, or upon society generally—but in these instances its effect may be more apparent.

Let me, then, ask if the destiny of the world so much depends upon the character of individuals as in the instance of Napoleon and of Washington—

and if that character of an individual is so moulded by the moral culture of his mind—let me ask if due attention is paid to this part of education in our common schools—I fear not.—I fear, that the field of morals is to our common schools a "terra incognita,"—and if any master has ventured so far from the shore as to discover this land, that he has not dared take his crew with him, to see its beauties.

Gentlemen, I should be glad to detain you longer upon the great interests involved in popular education—but I have occupied your attention too long already—one word more.—

There yet linger among us a few, who bore a part in the war of the revolution—may they late return to heaven—for we venerate them the more since their comrades are gone.—We value them as interesting relics of an interesting day, and like the Sybaline leaves we value them the more and more as their numbers grow less and less. For their sakes then, if for no other reason, let us go on—let us go on, encouraged by their example, animated too by the spirit of the age, and do all we can to fulfil the high destinies of our republic—let us further, as we yield up one after another, reluctantly, of this venerable band, do all we can, that their passage hence may be gladdened with the assurance that their virtues and their memory will live, engraven upon the hearts of a grateful posterity, forever.

Printed by Libri Plureos GmbH in Hamburg, Germany